To Jamie

Thanks for yo[ur]
support!

Best
C L[...]

YOURS & MINE

A WINNING BLENDED
FAMILY FORMULA

C. LYNN WILLIAMS

Cover Photo by C. Lynn Williams
Cover Design by Paper Butterfly Graphics

Published by 220 Publishing
(A division of 220 Communications)
PO Box 8186
Chicago, IL 60680-8186
www.220communications.com
www.twitter.com/220Comm

Library of Congress Cataloging-in-Publication data
Williams, C. Lynn
YOURS & MINE: A Winning Blended Family Formula
- C. Lynn Williams. – First edition
Pages cm
ISBN 978-1-5136-0481-7 Raising Children-Divorce-Remarriage-Parenting-Relationship 2. Women's Nonfiction. 3. Families. 4. Self-Help

ALSO BY C. LYNN WILLIAMS

Trying To Stay Sane While Raising Your Teen: A Primer for Parents, The Pampered Prince: Moms Create a *GREAT* Relationship With Your Son, and Raising Your Daughter Through the Joys, Tears & *HORMONES!*

FOREWORD

When I think of the amazing journey I have been on when it came to writing this book on blended families, I am reminded of how many different experiences had to occur and the people I had to meet in order to tell you this story. As you read on, you will see what I mean.

I want to thank my publisher, 220 Communications, for encouraging me to talk about this important topic of blending families and ways to keep the love in the relationship as well. Thank you Marisa Anstey, my editor, for guiding me to completion and tirelessly reminding me of my deadlines. Many thanks to my close friend, Carolyn Stewart, my husband, Jim, and my oldest daughter, Candace, for agreeing to read and reread these chapters until they all made sense. Thank you to the couples and individuals who agreed to allow their stories to be told: Jim and Susan Papandrea, Lorraine Cruz, and Herschenia and Mario Koonce.

Also thank you to my author friends on Facebook and those families who have graciously joined my private Blended Families Facebook group and don't mind sharing their daily struggles and triumphs.

-C. Lynn Williams

YOURS & MINE:
A WINNING BLENDED FAMILY FORMULA

By

C. LYNN WILLIAMS

Author of:
Trying To Stay Sane While Raising Your Teen
The Pampered Prince: Moms Create a *GREAT*
Relationship with Your Son
Raising Your Daughter Through the Joys, Tears & *HORMONES!*

220 Publishing

Chicago, Illinois
220 Publishing
(A Division of 220 Communications)

YOURS & MINE

A Winning Blended Family Formula

What is a *"blended family?"* It is a family consisting of a couple and their children from this (current) and all previous relationships.[1] When I envisioned this book, I was newly married to my second husband, so some of my perspective talks about dating and marriage. However, many relationships involve people who enjoy being together, are raising children from different relationships, and have no intention of marrying each other – but nonetheless are committed to each other and their family.

I came from a blended family. I was a teenager when my dad remarried a few years after my parents' divorce. It was awkward. She was a

---

[1] http://www.merriam-webster.com/dictionary/blended%20family

nice person, but in loyalty to my mother, I didn't like my step-mother. I am currently in a blended family where my husband and I had children from previous marriages. We have blended those children from different relationships into our family. We enjoy each other; more like tolerate each other, but we've grown quite a bit since our early encounters.

Forty percent of married couples with children (i.e., families) in the U.S. are step couples (at least in two-parent homes; 76% of Caucasians, 70% of Hispanics, and 42% of African Americans.) Thirty-five million Americans in the US today are remarried, with an additional 36 million Americans either divorced or widowed (possibly finding themselves in a remarriage at some point) (US Census, 2007.)[2] Twelve percent of women are stepmoms (14 million). This is only stepmothers (married or cohabiting) of children under 18 and

---

[2] http://www.smartstepfamilies.com/view/statistics

does not include stepmothers of adult stepchildren. Adding those women could double the estimate to 22–36 million.

Raising families today is pretty challenging, and staying happily married while raising children is very possible and can happen, provided you are willing to work at it every single day! Many years ago, societal pressures and religious beliefs kept people married to each other. Philandering husbands (or wives) were tolerated, alcoholism, drug and physical abuse still occurred, but people stayed in marriages because it was the "thing to do" or they stayed together for the "children." Today, blended marriages (with children) generally do not survive past five years. In fact, the blended marriage divorce rate is approximately 67%.[3]

The good news is that I know of at least five couples (including my husband and I) who have been married more than five years. The

---

[3]http://www.focusonthefamily.com/marriage/marriage_challenges/remarriage_and_blended_families.aspx

not so good news is that there is a different mindset now, whether it is the relaxed value system of our society, or the desire to have a better quality of life. People feel like this: "I won't stay in a love-less marriage like my mom did." The point is that many people decide to marry a wonderful man or woman and find themselves at the threshold of raising their children (from a previous relationship) with a new spouse. When that happens, all hell breaks loose! Loyalties change and that nice man or woman that you dated becomes **"THE ENEMY"** to your children! At least that's what my children said. How could I marry their friend, Mr. Jimmy? Well, all is not lost. You can marry Mr. or Ms. Right and stay happily married as well as confidently parent your children. It wasn't easy, but my husband and I are celebrating 13 years of marriage (by the grace of God no doubt.) Read on to discover our secrets.

TABLE OF CONTENTS

Part I – The Kids

Part II – Us as a Couple

Part III – Our Family

PART I
THE KIDS

This section is devoted to the beginning of your search for Mr. or Ms. Right. We talk about topics that matter to single and divorced parents who are interested in meeting someone wonderful to spend the rest of their life (and the lives of their children.) Your life is more complicated because the decisions you make not only affect you, but also your children. Getting involved with someone who is violent puts your lives in danger. Dating someone with addictive behavior either to drugs, alcohol, gambling, sex, you name it, will make your home life chaotic and unpleasant. Someone who stresses you out will also wreak havoc for your children, because while they may not understand what's happening, they will know "things aren't right" with mom or dad.

CHAPTER ONE
Dating Other People

At some point in your life as a divorced parent, you will want to date.

As I write this I realize that I have one or two friends who never dated

after their divorce. They are not the norm! Yes, there are exceptions,

but for the rest of us, you will eventually want to go out with some-

one who is not half your age or younger, compliments you because

you smell good, and notices that you are not wearing sneakers. There

is nothing like sharing milestones with a companion — sharing those

important dates like your child's graduations, Little League baseball

games, piano recitals, and your daughter's sweet sixteen birthday, or

your 30th, 40th, or 50th birthday. For some, the scars of divorce are so

deep that it takes years before the thought of dating crosses our

minds. For others, especially those who have young children, you hope that you can find love again and a spouse, who will help you raise your little darlings.

Dating was exciting and traumatic at the same time! Having been married for 18 years, I couldn't imagine sharing my life with another partner. Who would fit into my quirky family? What's odder than all of us climbing into bed together to watch "Home Alone?"[4] We had already established strong family customs and traditions that seemed pretty private. Odd I would think of that. However, I thought of that and much more before I started dating. Crazy, huh? Online dating wasn't as popular when I started dating, so it wasn't really an option for me, but I have friends who've tried it with success. I preferred meeting a guy through friends or family. Whatever your preference, take your time. Rushing makes you anxious and you may mistakenly date someone you don't like. If you are a person of

---

[4] http://www.imdb.com/title/tt0099785/

faith, pray about it. If you've read my other books, you know I believe that prayer changes hearts and circumstances. I wasn't interested in just dating; I wanted a life-long partner who I could share not only my dreams with, but who would also delight in the dreams of my children, as well as have me share his dreams and those of his kids.

By the way, do you have a crazy ex? Is this person going to show up at your house unannounced periodically? *Drama* with a capital "D!" We will talk about that a little later. While crazy exes are not a good reason to *NOT* date, they certainly affect if, when, and who you decide to date.

What kind of person are you attracted to? Does that person like children? Are they interested in the same things you like? Do you know what kinds of things you like? Do you like opinionated people or someone who likes everything you like? These are important questions because unless you want a parade of people coming in and out of your life (or the lives of your kids,) these are the things you might want to consider before you begin dating. I almost forgot to mention one more dating tip! Trust and safety. People are not always truthful when you date. They tell you what they think you want to hear and that can be an outright lie. For example, you ask, "Are you married?" They say, "No." What they mean is that they are thinking about divorcing their wife or husband, but haven't gotten around to telling them. You ask, "Do you have children?" They tell you no, but they don't tell you that they have two kids by two different women that they never bothered to marry.

These are just some of the pitfalls of dating. And here's another potential issue: If your instincts tell you to BEWARE, then beware. Before I went out on a date, I would tell my girlfriend or sister who I was going out with and where. I never felt like I was in danger, but I knew they would get in touch with the authorities if necessary. Always look to be safe, just in case. 🐦 #DatingOtherPeople

STUDY GUIDE QUESTIONS

DATING OTHER PEOPLE

1. Are you currently married and in a blended family? Explain your circumstances.

2. If you are single and raising children, what are some of the pitfalls you have faced?

3. What are your thoughts when it comes to dating and raising children?

CHAPTER TWO
When Do You Introduce Your Kids to Your "Friend"

Are you a protective parent? It's okay whether you are or are not.

There's no right answer. Here's my question: when is the right time

to introduce your "significant other" to your children? Is there a per-

fect time? I know comedian and author, Steve Harvey, believes you

should introduce your girl- or guy friend to your children right away,

because if you wait until you really like that person, would you be

prepared to walk away if your kids hate them? Good question! How-

ever, what do you do if you're not sure you like him or her? Do you

still introduce them to your kids? Couldn't the reverse happen?

Maybe your children will like him and you won't. Then what? An-

other fine mess . . . just kidding about the "fine mess." I am writing

these thoughts out because there is no guidebook when it comes to entering the dating/marriage game and raising your wonderful children with as little anxiety and trauma as possible.

Being a private person, I found it was easier to share my ideas and thoughts (and any new friend) once I had personally determined that they were worthy of meeting my son and daughter. I am sure that the decision you make on how to proceed is based on how you were raised. As I mentioned in my earlier books, my relatives were an extension of my parents, so everyone (mother, father, aunts, uncles, etc.) commented on the people I brought home. The person I brought home had to measure up to my family's standards. Having grown up that way, it makes perfect sense to me that the person I dated had to be pretty damn awesome in order to meet my children.

The real reason I would advise waiting until you are sure your date means more to you than a pack of gum, is because your children get attached easily to people who are significant in your life. Did I remember to say "Take it slow?" Take time to get to know the person you are dating. You don't have to run him or her through the FBI criminal database, but give yourselves plenty of opportunity to talk and find out about each other. People are pretty predictable and if you listen, they will tell you everything you want to know, and who they are. Wouldn't it be helpful to know that the guy you're attracted to is still married and has no intention of divorcing his wife? Or that the lady that you think is absolutely the best thing since sliced bread is a gold digger and only wants you around to pay her rent? Or perhaps after several dates – that means more than two – you discover that he is very critical and judgmental. Or maybe he is commitment-phobic and runs anytime he starts to have strong feelings for a woman. By the way, trust your gut. If you think something is wrong, it usually is. We have instincts for a reason and I trust mine implicitly. The longer you date without being intimate with each other, the keener your instincts. The keener your instincts, the better judge of character you are. If she tells you she doesn't like kids, don't think that she will change once she gets to know your kids. People seldom change, even when we want them to. So when you start to have urges of a sexual nature, tell your date to go home – alone! Unfortunately, sex clouds our judgment, and when that happens, we lose focus and perspective. Keep it platonic and you will hear the danger sirens going off, telling you to not invest any more time. Have sex before you're ready and you're on that emotional rollercoaster called "Love!"

🐦 #WhenDoYouIntroduceYourKids

STUDY GUIDE QUESTIONS

WHEN DO YOU INTRODUCE YOUR CHILDREN?

1. How do you feel about introducing your kids to the people you date?

2. Have you had a discussion with your children about dating people besides their biological father (mother)?

3. How long do you think you should date before you introduce that person to your children? Please explain.

CHAPTER THREE
Who Comes First – Your Kids Or Your "Friend"

This is not another trick question. This is easy! Your children always come first, well, after your spouse and God. We all say that, but it is often forgotten in the midst of chaos. Recently, I had a student whose mother kicked her out of their home, because she accused her stepfather of molesting her. Her mother was convinced she was making up stories about her new husband. How could you not believe your own flesh and blood – your own daughter? I suppose there are children who could make up stories like that, but you have to know your child. Are they a consummate liar and untrustworthy? Or have they always been pretty honest? Only you will know that. In any event, who was first in that mother-daughter relationship? Who comes first, your kids or your friend, when you are worried sick that your live-in boyfriend hasn't come home for three nights straight? I am sure that I am the world's biggest prude when it comes to live-in boyfriends. I don't believe in live-in boyfriends or girlfriends while you are raising children. However if my 'live-in' boyfriend stayed out for three days straight, he would be history! By the way, if your spouse or significant other is spending nights away from home, what does that mean to you and your children?

Think of it this way, unless your child is an adult, you have a moral and legal responsibility of holding everything together for the sake of your kids.

🐦 #WhoComesFirst

STUDY GUIDE QUESTIONS

WHO COMES FIRST?

1. When you were growing up, what kind of relationships did you see with your parents? Grandparents?

2. What kind of relationships did you observe with other family members?

3. In your mind, who comes first, the person you are dating or your children? Please explain.

CHAPTER FOUR
Daddy's Girl & Mama's Boy Woes

There are so many dynamics when it comes to allowing another person to enter the sanctity of your inner family of you and your kids. Many questions arise, such as: Will he like my kids? Will she treat them the way I would? How will he discipline my son or daughter? Will she treat my kids like she treats her own? Unless you are marrying someone with children under the age of two, children can destroy a relationship. What I mean is that children are geniuses when it comes to knowing the hot buttons of their parents. Plus, issues like "Will he like my kids?" would not occur if you didn't have children. I have heard men and women say "I don't want to date someone with children." There are a number of reasons why; however, the biggest reasons are that they don't want the responsibility, or they don't feel that they will be able to love someone else's kids as they would love their own.

Take discipline for example. There are hidden landmines when the unsuspecting spouse chastises daddy's princess or mama's little prince (even if the 'prince' is 16 or 17). You may get to see a side of your spouse or fiancé that you didn't know existed. Before you get to this point, it's good to talk about some key things, such as:

- Your parenting styles

- How you were raised

- What is respectful & what isn't (adults & children)

- Non-negotiables

- How you will parent together

- What to do when all else fails

Knowing each other's parenting style is important because wouldn't it be nice to know that the lady you fell in love with is the one who allows her kids to run wild in the mall because she hates to tell them no – it stifles their creativity! You, on the other hand, ruled your kids like a drill sergeant, so you consider her kids to be out of control. Whether this relationship is workable or not depends entirely on your ability to compromise and work with each other's parenting styles. How you were raised plays a big part in your style of parenting. When I was growing up, I swore I would never do things like my mother. The first time I heard myself say something my mom used to say, I couldn't believe it! Talking with your future wife or husband about the kind of things you won't tolerate from your kids is also important. Be prepared when he tells you that you have a blind spot when it comes to your son. "No, I don't!" you say. "Well, why doesn't he wash the floors? He's old enough," he says! You think, "I've always done it myself," but you retaliate with, "Why do you always give in to your daughter?" Great question, wrong timing! Honestly, it's a lot easier to have this conversation while you're dating and certainly before you have to deal with each other's kids. As

I was writing this, I thought about families like ours where custody was split. Sometimes our kids lived with us and other times they lived with their mother or father. We often didn't know we had a brewing problem until our kids were with us and the issue presented itself. It is also important to realize that the weekends that your kids are with your ex can influence your son or daughter in ways you aren't expecting.

I often felt that I had to undo the emotional 'noise' that my kids brought home after spending the weekend with their father. It may be as simple as your ex having more disposable income and being able to show your child a better time materially than you are able to. You resent having had to divorce, and find that you are saying mean things about your spouse to your kids. Whatever the issue, women tend to be more sensitive about comments made about their sons, and men are sensitive about comments made about their daughters.

What is considered respectful in one family could be reasons for punishment in another. My daughter was pretty outspoken and to other adults, sounded like she was disrespectful. Her father and I raised her to speak her mind in a respectful way. My current husband reminds me of how he felt at our first 'family' meeting when daughter dear spoke out about something that was important to her. He was surprised that I didn't send her to her room. For his benefit that evening, I reiterated the ground rules for our dinnertime discussion which were:

- No swearing

- No disrespecting yourself or each other

- No talking on the phone or texting during dinner

- No interrupting the person talking

Are you familiar with the Bible verse that talks about seeing the speck in your brother's eye, when there is a log in yours?[5] You will always see your significant other's children in a different light than you see your own. That's hypocritical and you will want to meditate to see each child equally. Fathers have a special spot in their hearts for their daughters. It's amazing how easily daughters wrap their fathers around their little fingers. As the new significant woman in your man's life, you have to proceed carefully in what you say about daddy's "little girl." I remember when Daughter #2 would call my husband, and if she sounded the least bit upset about something, he was out the door and on his way to help her. If there was a financial issue, he would do whatever it took to solve it. At the beginning of our relationship, it didn't matter whether our budget could handle the "issue" financially or not. It took a series of conversations (some

---

[5] Matthew 7:3-5 New Living Translation

gentle, some not so gentle) before he began helping her to confidently stand on her own. You see there was an emotional issue going on. My husband needed to feel that he was not abandoning his daughter for the second time. Second time, you say?? Many divorced dads feel that they've abandoned their children when they divorced their spouses. Sometimes the feelings of abandonment are self-imposed by the father because he no longer feels a need to stay close to his children (from his first marriage) as he is not involved with their mother. The other more widely recognized reason for abandonment is that the father has no money and feels that he's not a "real" dad.

Often daughters use their "daughter influence" to hijack their fathers financially. I call this an emotional hijacking because it may not make sense that daughters can say things like: "Daddy, if you really love me, you will send me to New York with my girlfriends," and the next thing you know, your husband has shelled out $500 for a plane ticket just because he doesn't want her to feel that because he loves you, he has stopped loving her (his daughter.) Often he may stop visiting his daughter altogether because he cannot provide those material things that he thinks she wants.

The same is true for mothers and those dashing darlings that they call sons. The one thing that often bothered my current husband was how close my son would stand to me. He felt like my son and I were joined at the hip. It felt natural to me, so I didn't really understand what he was talking about. I also know that I went into my personal savings and paid for my son to travel with his high school class to Costa Rica. While I am glad he had that amazing opportunity, the rational part of me wishes that I had made him earn the money to take the trip. It would have taught him the important lesson that he needs to earn, plan, and save for the things he wants, and I believe he would be further ahead in his journey to self-reliance. Both his father and stepdad disagreed with my decision. To learn more about my thoughts on mothers and sons, invest in a copy of my book, *The*

Pampered Prince: Moms Create a GREAT Relationship with Your Son
at Amazon.com.

Will you be able to avoid all the pitfalls of Daddy's Girl or Mama's Boy issues? Probably not, however, I hope this book, your fairy godmother of Blended Families, will tap you on the shoulder before you step into quicksand!

🐦 #DaddysGirlMamasBoyWoes

STUDY GUIDE QUESTIONS

DADDY'S GIRL & MAMA'S BOY WOES

1. Are you a single mother raising a son? If yes, please explain.

2. Are you a single father raising a daughter? If yes, what are some of the pitfalls you have faced?

3. How do you feel when someone criticizes your son (Moms)?

CHAPTER FIVE

Managing Your Time between Your Kids & Your "Friend"

Remember the first time you realized you were in love? You went out on a date, and when you got home, the two of you talked on the phone for hours. Had you not had to go to work the next day, you probably would have continued talking. You couldn't stop touching each other either. Remember?

Imagine having that same conversation with your children at home. How many times do you get interrupted? Every few minutes, right? I guess the down side is not getting interrupted at all. Maybe they don't interrupt at all because they are toddlers and they've gotten into something, like drinking water out of the bathroom toilet, or even worse, drinking the nail polish remover. Or maybe your time spent with your significant other allows your teen daughter to send sexting pictures to her boyfriend. I almost forgot; if your children are used to spending time with you, they will not be excited about sharing you with another person, especially one from the opposite sex. So what do you do? One possibility is if you share custody with your ex-spouse. I usually arranged dates when I knew my children would be spending the weekend or the day with their father. It helped me manage the guilt of being away from them. I tried to keep the long telephone calls to times when they were out with their friends or asleep. It didn't always work, but that was my norm. I also believed that it was important for my children and me to spend time with my significant other. Don't you like that phrase – significant other? It's so sophisticated, but beats calling them your boyfriend or girlfriend!

I think you get my point! It is difficult to carve time out with your sweetie; however, your kids come first. I remember when I decided to have sex with the man I was dating. It had been quite a while

before then, and I was like a kid in a candy store. A sugar rush!

🐦 #ManagingYourTime

STUDY GUIDE QUESTIONS

MANAGING YOUR TIME

1. You've met someone that you want to build a life with. How much time do you think is reasonable to spend with them?

2. How much time do you spend talking on the phone with him (her)?

3. How do you handle interruptions or 'acting out' episodes with your children? Please explain.

PART II

US AS A COUPLE

This section is devoted to you and your spouse. We will talk about topics that matter to the newly married couple and the wonderful opportunities that await you.

I call them opportunities, and you might call them challenges. It really depends on whether the glass is half full or half empty. You be the judge. You will learn more about each other every day of your life together. Some experiences you will be prepared for; others may take you by surprise.

CHAPTER SIX
You're Married, Now What?

Congratulations! You've stopped doubting yourself on whether this is Mr. or Mrs. Right for you. You've also made it past your son's or daughter's attempts to convince you that you shouldn't marry your beloved man or woman, whether it was because your daughter didn't like her hair color or your son thought he looked "mean".

Yes, it was rocky for a while, but your children have met his children; you've met your new in-laws and you have assured your ex-husband that your new husband is not trying to replace him as your children's father. Or maybe your ex-wife, who normally does not talk to you, has become very chummy and has started calling you once a week for one reason or another.

Now what? Have you thought about where you will ultimately live together as a family? When we married each other, my condo was slightly bigger than his, and my daughter was already enrolled in high school, so moving made no sense for us. His son (now our son) lived on his own, so we did not have to worry about having a bedroom for him except during his visits. His daughter (my new daughter) lived with her mother, so we could stay where we were for a while. The only problem was that my place was not large enough to accommodate all six of us when we were together. And, how do you call yourself a family when there is not enough living space for all of you? Years ago, I remember a family where the father had an adolescent daughter and married a woman who had three kids. They moved into a house that had enough bedrooms for everyone but the daughter. So she had to live with her great-grandmother. He explained that his daughter didn't really fit into his new family, and her life deteriorated quickly. Not being accepted as a member of his new family did a lot to ruin her self-esteem. I certainly didn't want that to happen in my new family.

Looking for a home together made sense not just because we wanted rooms for those who lived elsewhere. It was also important because it gave us a location that was neutral for both families. Even though most kids are naturally territorial, we felt our children couldn't be as territorial in a new place because none of us had occupied it before.

🐦 #YoureMarriedNowWhat

STUDY GUIDE QUESTIONS

YOU'RE MARRIED NOW WHAT?

1. What plans have you and your partner decided regarding living arrangements? Please explain.

2. What kinds of decisions have you and your partner made to help your children blend together more smoothly?

3. What (if any) areas of decision making are you not looking forward to and why?

CHAPTER SEVEN
Establishing Couple Guidelines

The wife of one of the couples that I spoke with mentioned that she wished she and her husband had waited to marry. When I asked her to explain, she said that her husband still carried a lot of baggage from his first marriage, and she felt that it affected their current relationship. Whether you marry the man or woman that you blend your family with, there is always a chance that one of you will carry baggage into the relationship. My husband used to say to me, "I am not like any man you've ever met." It was true, but hard to carry into our relationship, if something happened that reminded me of my former relationship.

In business, you are always asked to determine your goals at the beginning of the year. With your goals in mind, you have a better idea of gauging whether or not the steps you are taking are helping you meet those goals.

The same is true for your marriage. Instead of calling them goals, let's call them guidelines. Establishing guidelines allows you and your spouse to decide what you want from each other, and what you want from your children. You may decide that one of your guidelines is that if one mate says "no" to the child, the other mate will not say "yes." Another guideline could be that you will check with each other before making important financial decisions. A third guideline might be that you will not talk badly about each other to your respective children. Is it mandatory to set guidelines? Absolutely not! However, your goal is to stay happily married while you raise your brood together. If you have a set of guidelines (or rules) that you both agree to adhere to, you have a better chance of weathering potential landmines that could leave you angry with each other for days.

The major difference in this new relationship is that the issues that may cause you to walk away from each other are not necessarily comments from your parents or your best friends. Instead of having your mother-in-law constantly tell you what a screw-up your spouse is, your children could say, "Mom, why did you marry Joe? We hate Joe. He's mean to us." In your daughter's mind, she doesn't like Joe because he didn't allow her to hang out with her friends. Maybe it was a school night, or maybe he wasn't sure you wanted her out and since you were at work, he didn't have the chance to ask you. Kids are pretty clear about what they want and as a new family member, if you don't agree with the children, you can easily be cast into the "Mean Parent" pile.

🐦 #CoupleGuidelines

STUDY GUIDE QUESTIONS

ESTABLISHING COUPLE GUIDELINES

1. In which areas of your relationship with your partner do you want to establish guidelines? Please explain.

2. What kinds of guidelines would you like to establish regarding your children?

3. Is discipline one of the areas where you and your partner will establish guidelines? If not, why? Please explain.

CHAPTER EIGHT
How to Communicate Through Disagreements

Have you ever been really mad at someone? What did you do? How did you handle your anger? I don't know about you, but I simmer until I have a chance to talk about why I am angry. How long do I simmer? It depends on why I'm mad and with whom I'm mad.

It is pretty normal that, at some point, you will become angry with your husband or wife. While that is not a problem, how you communicate through your anger is very important. Staying happily married and being angry at your spouse don't match each other by any stretch of the imagination, unless perhaps you are thinking about the wonderful time you will have making up. ♥ Remember in the last chapter, we talked about establishing couple guidelines? Determining how you want to communicate with each other when you disagree is a great guideline to establish.

I remember leaving the house to clear my head a couple of times after disagreeing with my husband. That works if one of you is hot-headed and often says things that you later regret. It's hard to take back words said in anger. They leave scars, and depending on the scars you already have in your mental history, you don't want additional ones from your new relationship.

According to CodeName: Mama,[6] disagreements can lead to more "harmony and deeper connections." Why? Because disagreements give you and your partner an opportunity to become closer as you respectfully understand what it is your partner is saying and why they feel the way they do.

---

[6] http://codenamemama.com/2012/02/14/feb-2012-carnatpar/

Let's say, for example, that you are responsible for paying the household bills. Your spouse has a habit of using the household credit card and not letting you know. To make matters worse, it was a tight pay period and you get a message from your bank that your house account is overdrawn. Now you are mad! What do you do? Do you tell your partner how stupid she is? Or, do you give her the silent treatment? Answer this question first: how would you feel if the situation was reversed? Would you want to be yelled at, or even worse, be treated to a night of silence? Being the spontaneous person that I am, I would text a message to my partner right away. "Honey, we are overdrawn!" I would send a frown face with the text message.

It is probably not the best approach, but it is realistic and non-judgmental. I could have said, "Why didn't you give me your receipts? You've caused us to be overdrawn. Good grief, how in the world do you expect me to manage our money if you hold onto the receipts?"

See the difference? I am also spiritually attuned, so when I get annoyed with something my spouse has done, I declare "**Divine Order**" before I open my mouth. These two simple, yet powerful little words, have kept me from saying something insensitive or hurtful on many occasions.

🐦 #HowtoCommunicate

STUDY GUIDE QUESTIONS

How to Communicate Through Disagreements

1. Please explain what you do when you are angry.

2. Review the chapter and list a couple of ways you can communicate with your partner while in a disagreement?

3. List ways to communicate with your children (or your partner's children) during an argument or disagreement?

CHAPTER NINE
Disciplining Each Other's Kids

Where do you weigh in when it comes to discipline? Are you the type

of parent who talks to her kids when they've done something wrong?

Are you a tolerant parent? Do you let your children learn by their

experiences and mistakes? Or do you yell and scream? Do you spank

your kids? What kind of parenting style does your spouse have? You

will want to talk (in advance) about this very important topic, be-

cause no matter what style of parenting you or your spouse have, it

is difficult to hear the love of your life discipline your kids. If their

style is dramatically different than yours, it may be appealing in the

beginning of your relationship, but over time, may cause problems

between the two of you. It may be hard for you to listen to them

discipline your children, and your children may push back and try

not to obey or listen to what your spouse is saying. Supporting your spouse when he is correcting "the children" is definitely what you want to do, because it is the right thing to do. Kids are brilliant at knowing when there is a crack in the parental 'surface', and they take advantage when they believe their parents don't agree with the disciplinary measures that are taking place.

If one of you believes in spanking as a form of discipline and the other parent does not, this is an issue that has to be discussed and agreed upon in advance. The same is true if your method of discipline is yelling and cursing.

The other area that tends to be a problem is when the 'step' parent applies one form of discipline to your children, but not to her own. As I mentioned earlier, I knew a family where the husband had one daughter, and his wife had two sons and a daughter. When they found a house, it contained bedrooms for everyone but the husband's daughter. So she lived with her great-grandmother. That was completely unacceptable to me, and I couldn't understand what kind of dad would allow that to happen! If you are unfair in any area, you will lose the trust of your biological children, as well as your stepchildren. Once you lose their trust, it's hard to regain it.

One of the couples talked about how difficult it was to share discipline and share custody. When 'the kids' would come for the weekend, the parents would plan events and special meals. It didn't appear that the kids appreciated the money they spent or the activities that were planned. It was very frustrating! What they later found out was that the kids' mother would tell them how disloyal they were if they went to their father's house for the weekend and enjoyed themselves. So to keep a good relationship with their mother, they purposefully did not enjoy time with their dad and stepmother. Sad . . .

🐦 #DiscipliningEachOthersKids

STUDY GUIDE QUESTIONS

DISCIPLINING EACH OTHER'S KIDS

1. How were you disciplined as a child?

2. How was your partner disciplined as a child?

3. Are you comfortable correcting your children's behavior? Correcting your 'new' children's behavior? List a couple of ways you will correct their behavior.

CHAPTER TEN
Walking the Tightrope

Have you ever been to the circus and watched the trapeze artists? Those are the people who walk the tightrope high above the ground with those cute leather shoes and perfectly fit bodies! Well, I don't know about you, but walking a tightrope in life is pretty stressful, and as a mother in a blended family, I often find myself in situations where I am having to balance my relationship with my husband along with my relationship with my children. Maybe the situation is a secret that one of the kids has told me and asked me not to share. I really try not to have secrets from my sweet husband, because you have to remember what you promised not to tell, and at my age, remembering that I promised not to tell something is often as difficult as keeping the secret. Next it makes for spaces of discomfort in your relationship. The flow stops. Do you know what I mean when

I say 'flow'? Flow is the positive rhythm that you and your spouse have as you interact.

As I continue to work toward pampering my 'prince' less as he gets older, I think back on times when I probably overdid it as his mom. Not anything huge, but for example, knowing his weak areas and not pushing him constantly to be better, do more, achieve. It's not that we don't talk about those things and he knows that I expect the best from him. The issue is that his stepdad expects the same and more, and won't take "I couldn't make it happen" as an excuse. Walking the tightrope also occurs when you have to interact with your spouse's former wife, husband, or significant other. You want that interaction to be as positive as possible. There is no room for jealousy, anger, or resentment. You are involved with the man or woman of your dreams and working out the wrinkles to make sure that those exes are delicately handled is important to the smooth working of your relationship. Sometimes those conversations are necessary to ensure that there will be peace in your household.

The other time that I walk the tightrope is when my spouse tells me something about the kids that I'm sure he wishes I would share (with them), but I won't, and it creates noise in my head. I call it "*resentment*" noise. You know the noise you hear when fire engines are driving by beeping their horns and you feel like your head is going to explode? When I feel like that I look for words that describe how I feel about the "something" that he has said. There is no sense in internalizing stuff like that. Talk about it and stay happy with each other.

🐦 #WalkingTheTightrope

STUDY GUIDE QUESTIONS

WALKING THE TIGHTROPE

1. What does 'walking the tightrope' (in a relationship) mean to you?

2. In your relationship, who are you walking the tightrope with? Please explain.

3. List two ways you can minimize the stress that walking the tightrope means in your relationship.

CHAPTER ELEVEN
Ex-Spouse Drama

If I want drama, I go to the movies or watch reality TV. Actually I hate reality TV! Living with crazy, dramatic people is not my idea of fun. I like a quiet, peaceful household, which does not take place often when you are married and raising kids. So imagine adding an out-of-control ex-spouse to the mix! An out-of-control ex-spouse is one who constantly calls your house with different problems, stops by unexpectedly, or makes unreasonable demands. Maybe she constantly asks for money, or you find yourself in court more often than when you were a single parent.

Ex-spouse drama doesn't just occur between you and your ex. He might treat your children badly and you have to repair their self-esteem when they return to you after spending time with him. Your husband's ex might make it difficult to see your children on the designated weekend. Maybe she constantly tells your kids what a jerk you are or what a bad person their stepmother is. This will definitely cause conflict in your household. What do you do?

How badly it affects your children will determine what course of action you should take. If the drama is negatively affecting your children or spouse, talk to your children (spouse) first. Help them understand that your ex is reacting out of anger and hurt feelings, and that you hope that they will be able to move forward soon. Use it as a teaching opportunity to give other ways to respond when you feel hurt by someone. However, if the drama continues, try to talk calmly with your ex. If these tactics don't work, you may need to take legal action to modify the custodial agreement or enter an order of protection.

This is the person that is not happy that you or your new beau have found happiness with someone other than them. Never mind that you were not happy with them, or were separated for years; they still try to find a way to keep you or your children upset and out of sorts. My remedy is to ignore them (to the best of your ability) and treat them with kindness.

My grandmother used to say, "You get more bees with honey than you do with vinegar." It's true! Ex-significant others are caught off-guard when you don't react to their drama. At one point in our re-lationship, we were getting letters from attorneys, our wages were being garnished, and life was really tough for us. I also remember finding out that I would have my son for the rest of the summer, right after getting married.

I will tell you that trading bitter words will not cause the issues to stop. This is where having faith in a power higher than you is im-portant. We both prayed that the kids would hurry and grow up and they did. I also prayed that we would all (both ex-spouses) be able to get along with each other and enjoy the parenting of our children together. I don't have to tell you that prayer works!

🐦 #ExSpouseDrama

STUDY GUIDE QUESTIONS

EX-SPOUSE DRAMA

1. Do you have an ex-spouse? If yes, is there drama involved? Please explain.

2. List the two top issues that you face with your ex-spouse?

3. Below, write a note to your ex-spouse where you forgive him (or her) for the issues that he or she may have caused in your relationship.

CHAPTER TWELVE
In- & Outlaws

Have you ever heard of the in-laws from h*#@? I prefer to call them the **Outlaws**! Those are the relatives, often parents, who you inherit when you marry your spouse. I say inherit because they don't go away and they're often not nice people. If it's a mother who has not allowed her son to separate properly from her as he reached adulthood, then she will challenge everything you do. She will compete with you for your husband's affection, just like the mothers in the movies *Monster-in-Law* and *Jumping the Broom*.

Or it could be the doting father who is not pleased with you, his new son-in-law, because he doesn't think you will be able to take care of his daughter in the way he expects. Very much like the dad in the movies *Guess Who* and *Guess Who's Coming to Dinner*.

These kinds of relatives are tough to deal with, but over time seem to mellow once they see that both you and your spouse are quite able and comfortable taking care of each other (and your children). The other type of outlaw relative is the one who is just rude, bigoted, or manipulative. When this occurs, I suggest that both you and your spouse present a united front. Consistently support each other and don't allow yourselves to be manipulated into saying or doing something that you don't want to say or do.

My former father-in-law was a wonderful person (as far as I was concerned), but he gave my sister-in-law the blues because he didn't approve of her or her family members. He consistently gave them a hard time. From my viewpoint, it was his loss because he didn't have the best relationship with his children – or grandchildren. Unfortunately, walking on eggshells trying to make an in-law like you, probably isn't about you but more about their feelings.

🐦 #InOutlaws

STUDY GUIDE QUESTIONS

In- & Outlaws

1. Do your parents accept your partner? If not, please explain.

2. Is your mother-in-law friendly with you? Is your father-in-law friendly with you? Please explain your answer.

3. Do your in-laws have a relationship your children?

CHAPTER THIRTEEN
Date Night . . . Sex Anyone?

May I ask a personal question? What was it about your spouse or significant other that attracted you to him (or her?) Was it a physical attraction? Did they have money? Was it how they listened to you for hours while you talked about your dreams? Were they thoughtful, brought you gifts, cooked great meals, took long walks, and talked about future goals? Were they great in bed? Were they kind to your kids? When did you know that this was the man or woman of your dreams?

My husband and I were good friends before we started dating, but there was a lot that we didn't know about each other. We learned more about each other's values by spending time talking. The weekends that my children spent with their father were perfect times to grab lunch or dinner and just talk. I was cautious because I didn't want to ruin a perfectly good friendship, so there was no fooling around. But I noticed how kind he was and his values of relationship and family were the same as mine. I liked that. He was a great listener, too!

Those little thoughtful words, flowers, cards, gifts, and time together are what helped bring the two of you together. They are the same things (and maybe more) that will keep you delighted with each other. The only problem is continuing to make each other a priority.

How, you say? Schedule weekly date nights! Scheduling weekly time for each other gives you a chance to smile, talk, flirt; all of those things that keep love alive! Ideally your date night is time that the two of you spend away from home. Dates can be as frugal or expensive as your budget can bear. Dinner at an intimate restaurant, a baseball game, couple's massage, or a concert are examples of places you could go for date night. Change it up, too, so that each of you looks forward to the time together.

And, in case you've forgotten how wonderful you felt the first time you were intimate with your partner, keep the sex alive, too! I know you're tired – You've worked all day, cooked dinner, and helped your kids with their school projects. Or maybe you've closed a big deal with one of your clients, and have been burning the candle at both ends for at least a week getting ready for that presentation.

You're exhausted, right? Remember when he was the one that kept you up at night? He remembers, too! Don't lose touch with each other because of life's pressures. If you can afford it, get a "room" for one of your weekly dates. If a hotel room is not in your budget, put the kids to bed and take a luxurious bubble bath together with scented candles.

Oh, one more thing. If you are angry with each other and it is date night, be sure to have a relaxing glass of something wonderful to take the edge off of your disagreement and give you a chance to talk.

🐦 #DateNightSexAnyone

STUDY GUIDE QUESTIONS

DATE NIGHT . . . SEX ANYONE?

1. When you dated your partner, what kinds of dates did you have?

2. Now that you two have blended your families, do you still have 'date night'? If not, why?

3. Are you still intimate with each other? If not, why?

Part III

Our Family

This section is devoted to your life as a family, as you work at blending husband and wife with children from both relationships into a cohesive family unit. For example, your new spouse may have brothers and sisters with their own children that you want to introduce to yours. Also, his parents may be alive and well, and now your children have a new set of grandparents to share their life with!

"Are you my grandmother, too?" That's a question that children of blended families often ask the new grandparents. It was a question that both sets of my kids asked their new grandparents. It's confusing, because depending on family dynamics, they have known only two sets of grandparents: your parents and your spouse's parents.

When I remarried, my teens inherited a new set of grandparents. My in-laws were easy-going and my son and daughter were well-mannered, so deciding what to call them wasn't an issue, just different. "Call me Mama Brown; that's what all my grands call me." This is what my mother-in-law told my kids. My mother also had a nick-name that her existing grandchildren called her, so she invited my "new" son and daughter to call her that as well.

Each grandparent was as different as the name they were called. The biggest challenge wasn't "*what* to call" the new grandparents, but in blending our family in such a way that the awkward times were few.

I like the concept of a village raising a child, because it gives your child a rich texture of caring, related people to love and support them. Having three sets of grandparents, aunts, and uncles made a wonderful group of caring family members for my children to have in their lives.

CHAPTER FOURTEEN
Family Meeting

Don't laugh, but a smooth-running family has meetings just like any business. Did you not realize that a family was a business? The mom and dad are the executives and the children alternate between being employees and being stockholders. That's just my way of saying, depending on the situation, your children work for you (chores) and you work for them (by supporting them monetarily, emotionally, and mentally). Oh, and there are no golden parachutes ever. ♥

We had family meetings before I remarried, because I wanted to know what was going on with my children, and having family meetings allowed them an opportunity to speak without judgment or fear of being punished. Profanity and disrespect were not allowed at those meetings. Once I remarried, it was crucial to maintain the family meetings and to introduce my new husband into our family unit. When his children visited, they were included in the family discussions and encouraged to share any concerns that they had.

Often, the family meeting was just a discussion at dinnertime. It wasn't structured or scheduled; it just happened. The only ground rules were that we didn't answer phones or text during our meal. It was a time for us to learn more about each other. I will admit, if one of the kids had a problem that we knew about, dinnertime was tense and uncomfortable until we were able to talk! For example, one of our daughters was dating a guy that we didn't know much about. He seemed likable enough, but my instincts told me something wasn't right. Remember what I said about your instincts? Your instincts are seldom wrong!

We respected our daughter's choice of boyfriend, but when she didn't openly talk about this person, we asked what was going on with "Kenny." She told us that he was "okay," but we later found that Kenny wasn't trustworthy and was also a bully! (Goodbye Kenny!)

By the way, any family member can ask for a family meeting; they just have to say, "It's time for a family meeting." Just to show you how well the family meeting ground rules work, we are empty-nesters for the moment, and my phone rang during dinner one evening. To my husband's surprise, I answered it and talked to the person. He told me later that he could not believe that I answered the phone after all of our years of *"No Phones"* at dinner! He was right! What was I thinking?

🐦 #FamilyMeetings

STUDY GUIDE QUESTIONS

FAMILY MEETINGS

1. When you were a child, did your family conduct family meetings? Please explain what took place.

2. What are your thoughts about having family meetings?

3. Are you comfortable allowing your children and partner to talk openly during a meeting?

CHAPTER FIFTEEN
Household Chores

How you start is how you finish. What I mean is that if you start giving your children chores when they are young, and you are consistent with requiring that they complete the chores, as they become teens, there is a good chance that they will perform chores in their adult life. Responsibility can be taught by intentional parenting practices.[7]

It is amazing to me when mothers tell me that their son or daughter won't clean up their room, the kitchen, the bathroom, etc. Is this the first time you have assigned chores, or are you having a hard time consistently applying consequences if they don't complete the house-

---

[7] http://tip.duke.edu/node/745

hold chore? Here is my thought on household chores: everyone living in the house is responsible for making sure that it is clean and operational. Parents generally work to keep bills paid and make sure that there is running water, food to eat, heat, and electricity. As parents, that is our responsibility. If we are unable to do that due to physical or mental challenges, then we may have to rely on our adult children to assist us. Hopefully, physical or mental challenges won't occur while our children are young.

It is a great lesson in responsibility to teach our children how to clean their rooms, pick up after themselves, and as their age permits, start dinner, make grocery lists, wash dishes and laundry, dust and vacuum, take out the trash (including dragging the garbage can to the front of the house on the day of garbage pick-up), and budget. These are character-building responsibilities. First, it teaches self-reliance because the lessons you teach your child are never forgotten, and you can be confident that they will be able to take care of themselves once they leave home. Second, it teaches your child the importance of teamwork and how each member of the team has to do their part, in order for the family unit to be successful. Third, and most important, this lesson teaches your child that life is not all about them; you get further in life when you help others and allow them to help you.

So, when you and your spouse blend your families together, it is necessary to assign household chores and ensure that both sets of children complete them. It will be much easier if you are already comfortable with assigning chores to your own children. As you merge your families together, there is a Yours and Mine mentality. In our household, my children by marriage were convinced that I was the wicked stepmother assigning chores to them that my own children didn't have to do. One day, my youngest explained to his brother that "mom hands out these assignments to whoever is available, so you better do it." That sounds like a child who is used to working as a team member!

Do you remember the movie *Yours, Mine and Ours*[8], with Lucille Ball and Henry Fonda? Henry Fonda was a naval officer with 10 children and Lucille Ball was a nurse with 8.

As a naval officer, "Frank" (Henry Fonda) and his family were very comfortable with household chores; however, while "Helen's" (Lucille Ball) kids worked together, they had to be constantly reminded to complete their chores. If you haven't seen the movie, I won't spoil it by telling you how it ends.

But as entertaining as it was, it also showed the tedious side of parenting children from two entirely different families, generally raised with different parental requirements.

🐦 #HouseholdChores

---

[8] Yours, Mine and Ours, 1968 http://www.imdb.com/title/tt0063829/plotsummary?ref_=tt_ov_pl

STUDY GUIDE QUESTIONS

HOUSEHOLD CHORES

1. When you were a child, did you have household chores? Please list what they were?

2. If you did not have household chores, what are your thoughts about assigning chores to your children?

3. Do you show favoritism to any of your children? Your partner's children? Please explain.

CHAPTER SIXTEEN
There is No 'Step' in Children

My dad remarried when I was in my early twenties. I didn't get to meet his wife, my stepmother, until the night of the rehearsal dinner to my first husband. They lived in another state, so it was awkward to have my mother at an event with my dad and his new wife. I didn't like my new stepmother, and I'm sure I was unfair, but I didn't know her. She was pretty and my mom was sad. Eventually, my stepmom and I got to know and like each other, but my first memories of her were pure jealousy!

First of all, how could my dad go on and on about this woman? Did that mean he didn't love my mother anymore? Did he still love us? Anyway, the two things that stood out for me as I entered my new marriage: remove the label of 'step' from my vocabulary, and remember that while I loved my new husband, it didn't mean that my kids felt the same way. They had loyalties to their biological father.

The other side of 'step' is how you treat and introduce your spouse's children to your children. How do you introduce your 'newly acquired' children to other people, business associates, or strangers? Somehow, the word "step" sounds *second* class to me, and I don't like anything that feels like me or a member of my family are a second-class citizen.

I remember my husband introducing my son and daughter as his son and daughter. I liked that! If people who knew my husband's ex-wife looked puzzled, he would explain that they were his "stepchildren."

It took me more time to get acclimated to my new son and daughter. The more I practiced saying my sons and daughters, the better it sounded. I know I enjoyed having my oldest son call me "**Mom**."

He said it easily and it felt good. My youngest daughter compromised and called me "Mommy #2," which felt weird at first, but I understand loyalties all too well, so I was happy to be called Mommy anything. My kids and their friends call my husband by his first name. He encouraged it and they all seem to be comfortable with it. Early in our relationship, my kids didn't like how easily he accepted them into his life. I believe they felt it was somehow disloyal to their father. The main thing is for everyone to be as comfortable in a blended environment as possible.

🐦 #NoStepnChildren

STUDY GUIDE QUESTIONS

THERE IS NO 'STEP' IN CHILDREN

1. What are the ages of your children (your own and your partner's)?

2. What do your partner's children call you? What do your children call your partner?

3. How do you feel about the word "stepchild?" Please explain.

CHAPTER SEVENTEEN
Family Time Together

In each of my parenting books, I am a big proponent of spending time together as a family. It doesn't matter if your kids are young, pre-pubescent, hormonal teens, or young adults. Spending positive time together builds a family culture and great memories.

It is easier to create great memories together if you start when your children are young. They become used to picnics, family softball games, barbecues, museum visits, movie nights, or drives to the "country." If you don't start that type of tradition when they are young, it's not as comfortable when they become older kids. But. . . it's never too late. We love playing games together and going to the first showing of a new movie together. It doesn't matter that our kids are adults. Whichever kid is home when the newest superhero or sci-fi movie is released, goes with us to the movies for a night of fun.

If your budget is tight or non-existent, make snacks with your kids, and play games like *Monopoly* (yes I know that's so old school) or *Apples to Apples*© or *Phase 10*© or *Scrabble*© at home. I like games where you can include everybody, have healthy competition and lots of fun. If you have builders in your family, create a dollhouse, tree-house, model car, or whatever you want, as long as it involves inter-acting with as many people in your family as possible.

Before I remarried, I dated a man whose daughter was a teenager. She chose not to attend our family (and, yes, I considered him fam-ily) outings, although she was invited. He often mentioned how much he enjoyed our concept of family time together and wished that I had been his daughter's mother. Cool, huh?

Family time fosters conversation and good feelings. It builds a community of trust within your nuclear family, and shows your children how to create traditions that they can share once they begin having their own family.

🐦 #FamilyTimeTogether

STUDY GUIDE QUESTIONS

FAMILY TIME TOGETHER

1. As a child, what kinds of activities did you and your family do together?

2. What does family time consist of today with you, your partner, and your children?

3. Does family time mean that you have to spend money to enjoy yourselves? Please explain.

Epilogue

As I complete this book about *YOURS & MINE: A Winning Blended Family Formula,* I think about how easy it is in our society to give up, walk away, and stop trying to keep a loving relationship alive. It doesn't matter whether it is a relationship between adults or one between parents and children. I get it that adults can have irreconcilable differences, but when that relationship involves children, you really cannot divorce children.

Marriage and parenting is not for the faint-hearted. People that I respected often said this to me and I am sharing these same words with you. Those marriage vows have to mean something besides infatuation, money, and good looks. Each eventually passes away. Parenting is a life-time commitment. Sometimes, the adult children need more of your time (as they go through challenges and life experiences) than your younger children do. Be willing to share your time, your resources, and your love. Allow your children to make mistakes. It's hard to watch, but it really helps them grow exponentially!

I hope you have enjoyed reading this book as much as I've enjoyed writing it. As you read each chapter, let your friends on social media know by using the hashtag at the end of each chapter – Example ➔ #BlendedFamilies or #UsandThem

I welcome your thoughts and comments.

Stay in touch with me by email me at: clynn@clynnwilliams.com. Follow me on Twitter & Instagram @MsParentguru. I'd love for you to follow my *Staying Sane* parent blog, too: http://author-clynnwilliams.wordpress.com

Best wishes,

C. Lynn Williams -aka- #MsParentguru

🐦 #BlendedFamilies Rock!

What Others Are Saying About C. Lynn Williams:

"C. Lynn Williams really knows how to show her audience how to believe in your dreams and to continue to elevate in your life with continuous persistence and hard work. C. Lynn takes topics about Raising Teens, Keeping Marriages together, and other social issues that many people are not willing to discuss in a positive manner.

Not only does C. Lynn discuss these social issues, she provides you with many sources and data to help us all learn more about being a better individual, parent, and communicator to our loved ones. I have personally read *Trying to Stay Sane While Raising Your Teens* and *Raising Your Daughter Through the Joy, Tears and HORMONES.* Using some of her suggestions from these two projects has changed my life in parenting and being a better person overall. I look forward to reading her new project, *YOOURS and MINE: A Winning Blended Family Formula* in its entirety. I strongly suggest anyone who is seeking an honest and heartfelt way to deal with daily issues should RUN out and purchase all of C. Lynn Williams' projects."

-Anthony D. Collins, Author & Talk Show Host

www.anthonydcollins.net

"I have taken a glimpse inside of C. Lynn Williams' book and I must say she's dead on! She addresses some of the issues that single and divorced parents face when looking to reenter the dating scene. There is so much to consider and so many potential pitfalls that a parent must be aware of before starting the dating process. For me, after ending an 18-year marriage and deciding to get remarried 2 years later, the challenge of blending his family with mine was very real and ALL of our children were over 18, some into their 30's!

For your children, it is never the right time for you to date or re-marry, so you have to decide for yourself. Ms. Williams helps you to figure out what's important to you in a relationship and as a parent. If you are unsure about whether to start dating (or not), C. Lynn Williams' book will give you the insight you need to make the right decisions for you and your family."

-Toni Harris, "The Turnaround Queen"

"I remarried seven years ago, and never considered the dynamics of a new husband and my two children from my previous marriage. We dealt with issues such as: What should the kids call my husband? Is it okay for my husband to discipline? And, with whom should they spend Father's Day? Thankfully, with time, patience, and a lot of prayer we have become our own very special family, and a family with a very strong bond. Most people don't know we are a blended family not only because of the love shared between us that reaches beyond biology, but because we made the conscious choice to love with no boundaries and to communicate our feelings openly and to know they are valid and safe.

Blended families are very special and if you make the choice to accept and love regardless of DNA, I have no doubt your family will thrive and create long-lasting memories of a lifetime just like mine. The work is daily, but the rewards are worth a lifetime!"

-**Christie R. Edwards**

CPSIA information can be obtained
at www.ICGtesting.com
Printed in the USA
FFOW01n1858121115
18512FF